IMAGES OF WALES

MID-RHONDDA
FROM PENYGRAIG
TO LLWYNYPIA

Contents

The Swan Hotel, Penygraig, *c.* 1906. The landlord standing at the main entrance to the hotel is Mr Edward Thomas Morris, together with his young son. Mr Morris was the landlord of this hotel from 1891 to 1910.

Acknowledgements

The author would like to thank the large number of people who helped in the compilation of this book. Without their assistance the book would not have been published. I apologise to anyone whose name has been omitted from the following list: Mr Ken More (Porth), Mr Clive Davies (Victoria, Australia), Mr Hayden Shadbolt (Trealaw), Mr Clive Hughes (Tonypandy), Mr Bernard McTiffin (Trealaw), Mr Brian Richards (Trealaw), Mr and Mrs Vince and Caryl Warren (Tonypandy), Mr Len West (Trealaw), Mrs Ann Woodington (Penygraig); Mr Thomas Nicholas (Trealaw); Mr Peter Phelps (Tonypandy).

Last but no means least, I would like to thank Mr Owen Vernon Jones (Penygraig) for his excellent introduction and poem.

Introduction

The social scene of an area develops out of economic conditions and these conditions have changed dramatically in Rhondda over a relatively short period of time. We can therefore expect the way we once were in Rhondda to be very different from the way we are now. A sparsely populated rural area with little social intercourse was transformed into a heavily industrialised one with an instant population. There were rich social effects. The cause was coal. With the disappearance of the industry our valleys have been transformed once again and have become residential. David Carpenter's book is a pictorial record of society in coal-mining Rhondda.

Standards of living have improved in so many ways – in hygiene, mobility and means of communication. Entertainment is now ready-made, without the need to leave the house. Yet one cannot help marvelling at our once tight social cohesion. There were so many occasions, so many organisations which brought us together in expression of shared interest and neighbourliness.

David Carpenter's book embraces postcards, formal photographs and snapshots. His search for them is insatiable and is evidence of his inexhaustible energy and enthusiasm. He is ready to travel to locate a photograph or to seek an interview. It is a labour of love to him and we are indebted to him for enabling us to share it. This book reflects an age, but it is for all time.

Mae rhaid i ni ddiolch David Carpenter am helpu i ddangos i ni, trwy ei luniau, hanes gorffennol y Rhondda.

Owen Vernon Jones

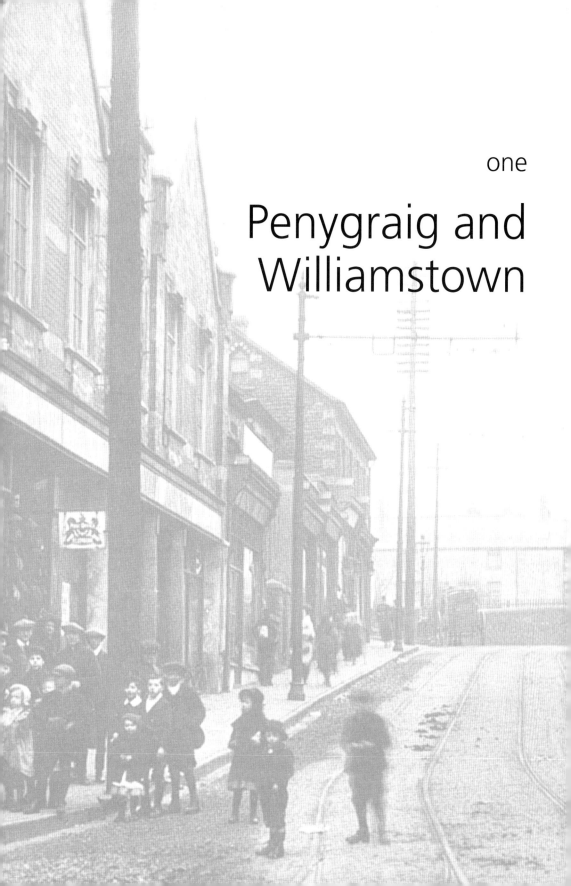

one

Penygraig and Williamstown

Naval Colliery, Penygraig, 1920. Opened in 1879 by Moses Rowlands Jnr, the number of miners employed in the colliery in its heyday exceeded 2,000. However, due to the reduction in the demand for coal the colliery closed in 1958. Part of the site was developed in 1967 with the construction of the Graig Park Rugby Ground, home of Penygraig Rugby Club.

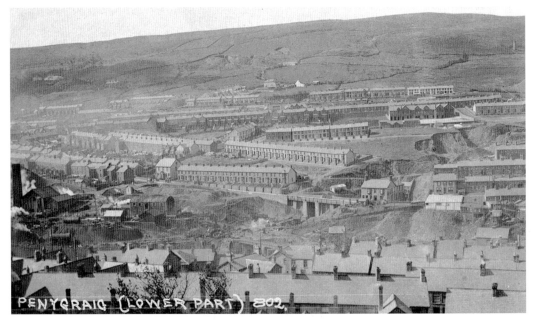

View of the lower part of Penygraig in 1910. Note that the Adare Inn is situated near to the bridge over the incline taking the colliery waste to the tip on the top of the mountain.

Penygraig Rugby Club

The story of the formation of the Penygraig Rugby Club goes back to the 1870s, or perhaps even earlier. It has been told that at this time the son of the proprietor of the Butcher's Arms in Penygraig, Morgan Rees Jnr, returned home from college with an oval-shaped ball, something which had never been seen in the Rhondda at that time.

Legend has it that a brother or cousin of Morgan Rees, the proprietor of the Butcher's Arms (and the father of Morgan Rees Jnr), kicked the first rugby ball in the Rhondda – through the window of the Butcher's Arms Hotel.

This peculiarly shaped ball aroused such considerable interest with the local youngsters that they started to play with it and, through the encouragement and backing of Morgan Rees Jnr's mother, Mrs Rachel Rees, and despite opposition from various religious bodies of that time, a side was formed which gave birth to Penygraig Rugby Club, one of the oldest clubs in Welsh rugby.

The first recorded rugby match was against the Maritime and took place at Ynys Field, with the newly formed Penygraig team being the victors.

While it would appear that they played many of their matches at Ynys Field, Penygraig also played numerous games on other grounds such as Belle Vue Park at the top of Dinas mountain and Llestwyn ground in Penrhiwver, as well as the new mid-Rhondda ground, as the sport gained popularity throughout the district. The season of 1886 appeared to be the time when Penygraig made an impact on the sport in the Rhondda and District League.

In the 1887/88 season Penygraig proved themselves on the field by defeating such teams as Cardiff, Newport and Llanelli, as well as many other premium sides.

In 1889 one of the greatest achievements in the history of the club took place when they won the South Wales Championship Cup. Again in 1906 they played Mountain Ash and defeated them to win the Glamorgan League Cup.

Success followed success, and the reputation of the Graig spread, with the club becoming regarded as one of the foremost in Wales.

During the 1920s the Welfare Park, Penygraig became the home ground and remained so until 1970. In 1961, the new and current clubhouse was opened in what had been the local colliery manager's house at Tylacelyn Road, Penygraig, and it was due to the tremendous efforts of the club officials at that time, that is, Mr Gwyn Williams and Mr W.D. Jones, that the procurement and development of the new Graig Park ground took place.

The opening of this ground took place on Tuesday 1 September, 1970, and was celebrated when the Graig played Newbridge on the new ground.

Over the years, further developments and successes have taken place, with the club playing host to a number of international touring teams as well as first-class sides, with the result that Penygraig Rugby Club is well known and respected throughout the rugby world.

Above: Penygraig Rugby Football Club, 1906, winners of the Glamorgan League Cup in the 1905/06 season.

Opposite: Aerial photograph of the newly developed Graig Park Rugby Ground, home of the Penygraig Rugby Club, which was opened in September 1970. The first floodlit match played on this ground took place in October 1970, between Penygraig and Pontypridd.

Penygraig Rugby Football Club, Portugal Tour, 1990. From left to right, back row: Ceri Jones, Jeff Jones, Simon Richards, Ian Griffiths, Robert Harrison, Neil Wilcox, Ian Woodington, Nigel Hendy, Ian Bailey, Scott Eggar, Phil Lott. Front row: Andrew Harrison, Meirion Harrison, David Foley, Roddy Woods (Capt.), Gary Davies, Robert Llewellyn, Alun Pope, Richard Davies, Simon Mellor.

Tylacelyn Road, 1904. Note the absence of traffic except for the single horse-drawn cart!

Hendrecafn Road, 1908. The houses on the right were occupied by professional and business people of Penygraig.

Shopping at Ffrwdamos Square in 1904.

THE SQUARE, PENYGRAIG. 153.

A quiet Ffrwdamos Square in 1908.

The view from Ffrwdamos Square, 1910. Note the development of the shops and the new tram lines.

Ffrwdamos Square on a busy day in 1911. Note the tram plying its trade from Tonypandy to Porth.

A typical Sunday School outing organised by Sidney Davies in the 1950s.

Form 2 pupils at Graig Yr Eos School, 1947.

The Vicarage, Penygraig, *c.* 1910. It is now converted into two houses.

Penygraig Park, seen here in 1926, was built for the local community and opened in November 1912.

Cenotaph, Penygraig.

The Cenotaph in around 1920, which was erected in the Park in memory of those who fell in the First World War.

A view of the Ely Colliery, 1920. A dispute at this colliery in 1910 led to the General Strike in the South Wales Coalfield and the famous Tonypandy Riots of 1911.

Brook Street, 1910. At that time, Brook Street was one of the main streets into the Rhondda.

A view of Brook Street, 1910. Note the absence of tram lines at that time.

A view showing the Welfare Park situated across the main railway line, 1937.

A view of Penygraig and mid-Rhondda, 1937. Note the stacks of the 'Scotch' Colliery in the distance.

The Pimmer in around 1910, leading to Vicarage Road. Note Tai School on the left, and the White Rock Hotel on the right.

Penygraig in 1951. Note the removal of the spoil from the tip, bottom right This area became the official ground for the Penygraig Rugby Club.

Williamstown Primary School Football Team, 1955/56. Team members are: B. Price, R. Crichton, L. McPhail, D. Humphreys, Alan Evans, G. Button, Ken Stone, J. Thorne, G. James, R. Davies, B. Mathews, T. Rees, D. Morgan, and G. Jones. Seated are teachers Mr Hughes (left), and Mr Harding (right).

Class 4B at Williamstown Primary School, 1946.

The Golden Age Hotel, *c.* 1942. The hotel was originally opened in 1906, its landlady being Mrs Mary Howells. It has since been demolished.

Situated on the boundary of Williamstown, the Lewis Arms, which opened in 1871, was very popular with the inhabitants of the area. Its first landlord was Jenkin Thomas. It closed in the early 1980s and was later demolished under a road-widening scheme.

two

Trealaw

The new Passenger Railway Station serving Tonypandy and Trealaw, *c.* 1910.

The Trealaw Salvation Army Band, 1907.

Trams plying their trade in Miskin Road, Trealaw, *c.* 1910.

Miskin Hotel, Trealaw, *c.* 1912. The landlord at that time was Mr Albert Griffiths.

Lower Brithweunydd Road, Trealaw in 1908. Note the tram in the distance.

Pupils of Alaw Primary School, Trealaw, 1913. The headmistress (on the left) was Miss John, and the class teacher of forty-nine pupils was Miss Evans (on the right).

Members of All Saints' Church Drama Society, Trealaw, in 1931. The vicar at that time was Revd W.H.H. Williams.

Members of All Saints' Church Mothers' Union, Trealaw, preparing for their annual charabanc outing in around 1938.

31

Fête at Maes Yr Haf in aid of All Saints' Church funds, *c.* 1918. In costume from left to right, back row: Harold Watkins, Warren Squires, Sid Baker, Freddie Parker, -?-, Percy Waite. Front row: Ivor Davies, -?-, Emlyn Gwilym, Oliver Davies, Trevor Griffiths.

All Saints A.F.C. during the 1948/49 season, when they were Rhondda League Division One champions. They were also Ely Valley Cup winners. From left to right, back row: J. Holloway, R.J. Pugsley, D.K. Davies, L.C. Evans, D.J. Hopkins, G. Rays, G. Richardson, H. Savage, L.G. Edmunds, J. Gilbert. Middle row: M.T. Thackwell, -?-, B. Thackwell, A. Richardson, Mog Morgan (coach), Revd G. Watkeys, M. Savage, V. Bailey, E. Bailey. Sitting: Norman Jones, Keith Tovey (mascot), Mervyn Holloway.

Quilting class at the Maes-Yr-Haf in the 1960s. From left to right, back row: –?–, Mrs Owen, Mrs Poultney, Mrs Powell, Mrs Davies, –?–, Mrs Bailey, Mrs Thomas, Mrs Richardson. Middle row: –?–, Mrs Hallet, Mrs Bright, Mrs Griffiths, Mrs Naylor, –?–, Mrs Smith, Mrs Blake, –?–, –?–, –?–. Front row: –?–, –?–, Mrs Selwood, Mrs Lee, –?–, Mrs Williams, Mrs Perry, –?–.

Trealaw Park Bowling Team, 1946. Team captain was Mr Olive Davies (centre), the owner of 'Checks' stores.

A view of Garth Park, Trealaw, 1945.

Bill Davies and his son Ron with one of their new fleet of delivery lorries at the Excelsior Works, Trealaw, in 1965.

A group of workers outside the Excelsior Works, known throughout the area as 'Davies' Pop Factory', in 1965. From left to right: Ron 'Pop' Davies, Edith Jones, Gladys Davies, Dorothy McTiffin, Maisie Jones, Iris Roach, Doreen Flanders, and Bill 'Billo' Davies.

The Excelsior Works, Trealaw, was opened in 1921 and named after the brass band from the Forest of Dean of which the founder of the works was a member. It remained open until July 1987, when its equipment was shipped to Nigeria. The buildings were demolished and two large dormer-type houses built on the site.

A group of unemployed miners at the Old Mineral Water Works prior to it being converted to the 'Don'. The photograph dates from around 1934–35.

Alaw Nursery School, opened in 1938, provides accommodation for 200 infants between the ages of two and seven years. It was officially opened on 21 December 1939 by Councillor Mark Harcombe, Chairman of the Building Committee.

Dinner time at Alaw Nursery, 1939.

A children's party at Alaw Nursery School, 1951. The headmistress, Mrs Howells, is in the background, together with Mr Noel Davies, headmaster of Trealaw Junior School.

Members of the Mothers' Fellowship at Trealaw Nursery School, c. 1950. They provided the teachers with mutual assistance in dealing with problems involving child welfare needs at that time.

Alaw Junior School, c. 1970. The headmaster, Mr Noel Davies, is on the left, and the deputy headmistress, Mrs Price, is on the right.

Teaching staff at Alaw School, 1949. From left to right, back row: -?-, Gladys Davies, Gladys Thomas, 'Pa' Lewis. Front row: A.M. Price, Mr. J. Lewis (headmaster), -?-.

Nine sets of twins at Alaw Junior School in 1961–62. From left to right, back row: Janice and Gerald Razey, Clive and Allan Hughes, Jeff and Graham Coles, John and Ann Mountford. Front row: Doug and David Wright, David and Margaret Davies, Diane and Doreen Spearing, Susan and Wendy Evans, Royston and Russell Bridge.

Above: Alaw Juniors Football Team, 1988, sponsored by Trealaw Social Club (The Res). From left to right, back row: Mr Davies and Mr Emanuel, teachers and trainers. Middle row: Kevin Barnett, Alun Evans, Andrew Sacket, Scott Wait, Jamie Jenkins, Geraint Higgins, Dean Williams, and Neil Jenkins. Front row: Rhys Davies, James White, Andrew Llewellyn, Mathew Baker, Christian Roach, Kevin Brough and Graig Griffiths.

Opposite above: Cemetery Road, Trealaw, *c.* 1930. Note the buckets of ashes out on the pavement for collecting.

Opposite below: The Queries Concert Party, 1926. From left to right, back row: Bill Phillips, Cyril Roddy, Oliver Davies. Front row: -?-, -?-, Tom Phillips, -?-.

CEMETERY ROAD,
TREALAW

Above: The interior of 'Checks' stores, 1933. When you consider that the shop consisted of the front room of a dwelling house, one marvels at the amount and variety of goods that are displayed for sale.

Right: The staff of 'Checks' stores, *c.* 1928. They are Mrs Maggie Davies, Miss Abbie Luker and Miss Sarah Luker.

Opposite: Bottom 'Checks' stores, *c.* 1920. The manager standing in the doorway is Mr Dan Griffiths, whose father, Mr William Griffiths, was the landlord of the Halfway House Hotel, Dinas, which had been closed and demolished around 1910. The name of the boy customer was ? Jenkins.

Residents of Marjorie Street, Lower Marjorie Street, and Brynteg Terrace enjoying the Victory in Europe celebrations in May 1945.

A view of Trealaw Cemetery in 1935. In the foreground, the construction of the Dinas playing fields is taking place. This ground was officially opened by King Edward VIII during his visit to the Rhondda in 1936.

Cemetery Church, Trealaw.

The church at Trealaw Cemetery, *c.* 1908. The church was built in 1881 and its high steeple was lowered a few years later due to high winds causing structural damage. After years of neglect it was completely renovated in 1994.

Three of the four-strong team of grave diggers at Trealaw Cemetery *c.* 1958. From left to right they are: Tommy ('Nick') Nicholas, Bob ('Left Hand') Owen, and Syd Towell. A fourth member of the team, Malcolm Harries, was acting as the photographer. Syd became Sexton in 1964, and retired in 1980. Tom became Sexton in 1980, and retired in 1996.

Trealaw Social (The Res) Football Team, 1968. From left to right, back row: Brian Richards, Alan Morgan, Ken Stone, Jeff Howells, Brian Walby, Gary Thomas, Paul Gubbins, Val Hughes. Front row: Ken Morris, Norman White, Ken Jones, Alwyn White, John Gimson, Brian Jakeway, and Glan Jones.

Members of Trealaw Social Club (The Res) preparing for their day out at Newbury Races, *c.* 1987. They are: Terry Davies, Hywel Morgan, Mervyn Israel, Tony Griffiths, Eric Groves, Russ Thomas, Glyn Wornell, John O'Leary, Les Wills, Tommy 'Khyber' Davies, Ken Stone, Ron Tovey, Des Underhill, Brad Bunstowe, Fred Coombes, John Bills, Adrian Joseph, Dilwyn Edwards, Les Woods, Glan Jones, and Bryn Hopkins.

Members of the Cork Club at the Bute Hotel, Trealaw, warming up for their forthcoming trip to Ireland in 1962. Unfortunately this was cancelled due to the smallpox epidemic which occurred at that time. From left to right, back row: Len Vincent, Dave Trott, Wilf Rees, Graham Dando, Omrey Evans, and Hywel Morgan. Middle row: Doug Jones, Gordon Bridge, Adrian Dando, Brian Owen, and William Henry Rees. Front row: –?–, David Brown, Jack Martin, Brian Richards, David 'Minto' Griffiths, and Selwyn Thackwell.

Members of the Woman's Guild at Trealaw Social Club enjoying themselves on a weekend trip to Blackpool in 1958. Among those who attended were: Mrs Y. Mathews, G. Hughes, G. Bailey, F. White, O. Pring, ? Bully, O. Harcombe, ? Bright, G. Roach, F. Jinks, J. Griffiths, I. Roach, R. Bright, D. Morgan, N. Johnston, S. Clarke, ? Poultney, P. Jones, ? Owen, V. Joiner, ? Carbines, W. Jones, D. Griffiths, ? Griffiths, Z. Lewis, and N. Harding.

Regulars at the Bute Hotel, Trealaw, enjoying the Christmas celebrations in 1997. They are Will Parker, Gerald Underhill, Sid Hurket, David Evans, Brian Richards, Sid Jenkins, David Griffiths, Lenny Vincent, Alcywn Powell, John Prosser, David Hopkins, Ken Hopkins, Idris Walters, Jim Kenedy, John Griffiths, Gordon Jones, Terry Blinkorn, and Trevor Carpis. The landlord at that time was Mr Gibbons.

three

Tonypandy

Pre-War Pandy

O to be on Pandy Square
When shop lights all were on,
To watch the crowds of people there.
Now sadly all are gone.

They walked, they talked, they jostled
In Pandy's bright parade.
They joked, they laughed, they flirted.
Those memories never fade.

The Square was marked so clearly
By the Lady with the Lamp,
Standing on the horse trough
That stood upon a ramp.

They queued outside the Picturedome.
The queues were long and deep,
Waiting for the second house,
Bright dreams before they sleep.

The café doors were open
With smells that filled the air.
Students used them often then.
The atmosphere was rare.

The pub doors were open.
Welsh voices filled your ears
Colliers drank there now and then
To down a local beer.

And there you heard so close at hand,
The Salvation Army's own brass band;
Carrying its message to all around
A joyful and triumphant sound.

And through the crowd the tramcar
Rocked its sparkling way.
'Be careful of your backs, dears
You're standing in its way!'

Owen Vernon Jones

Tonypandy Square, 1904. Note the absence of the 'Lady with the Lamp' fountain, a memorial to the late Archibald Hood. This was erected in 1909.

The Pandy Inn was built around 1861, its first landlord being Thomas Williams. It was rebuilt about 1900, its landlord at that time being Thomas Morris, and the inn became a firm favourite with the people of the area, especially with the miners who used to call there after their shifts in the local collieries.

After modernisation and redecorating in 1991, a plaque relating to the Tonypandy Riots was mounted on the wall of the inn. This was appropriate, as during the miners' strike in 1910–1911, the inn was a focal point where the striking miners congregated.

When it was first built, this inn was used as a Local Court by visiting magistrates to impart justice, and is one of the main reasons that streets and houses in the locality are named Court Street, Court Place, Court House, Cwrt Terrace, (the huts built in 1862) etc. Prior to the building of the inn, and under the Feudal system in existence at that time, people came from different parts of the locality to transact civil (and indeed criminal) business relating to the Court of the Manor of the Lordship of Glyn Rhondda. This took place on a large mound at a field called Ynys-Y-Crug or the Field of the Mound (near the inn). Today it is only a fragment of its original size, and can be seen at the side of the new Tonypandy bypass.

Local farmers served as petty constables in those times until the first policeman was appointed in 1837, when he dispensed justice with the full authority of the law. (Perhaps this led to the term 'petty sessions' used by the Local Courts). The petty constable was employed for the maintenance of order and the enforcing of the laws. In the parish of Ystradfodwg, the petty constable was the officer of the court leet of the Manor of Clynrhondda. He made his presentments to the court, which had to be held twice a year, in May and October. The petty constable was not paid any wages and was obliged to keep law and order and to make arrests for a period of six months. This was in addition to his

Tonypandy Square, 1933. Note the positioning of the fountain, and the alterations to the Pandy Inn.

own job at the time. When his six-month term was over he then returned to his normal job and another person was forced to take on the job for a further six months. His badge of office was a heavy staff which was hung on the door of his house, thus distinguishing his house from the others in the area. Today the inn is still a very popular venue, especially with the younger generation.

The Tonypandy Square Fountain (the 'Lady with the Lamp')

On Thursday 28 October, 1909, Mr W. Abraham (Mabon) MP performed the unveiling ceremony of the magnificent drinking fountain erected to the memory of the late Archibald Hood JP, founder of the Glamorgan Collieries. This fountain was purchased and erected out of the surplus monies which were subscribed by workmen and others for the erection of the imposing statue which stands in the grounds of the Workmen's Institution at Llwynypia.

The fountain, which is 13ft high, is built of cast iron on a pedestal of Aberdeen granite, and is surmounted by an Egyptian water carrier supporting a powerful gas lamp. It had three drinking taps, one cattle trough, and two dog troughs. It was built by the Coalbrookdale Company from designs by Mr R.S. Griffiths, architect, Tonypandy, and bore the following inscription:

> 'This fountain was erected in conjunction with the statue at the Workmen's Institute by the workmen of Llwynypia Colliery and others as a memorial to the late Archibald Hood Esq., JP and founder of the Llwynypia Collieries.'
> There was also the following in Welsh: 'Y cyfiawn a fydd ofalus am fywyd ei anifail (Diar. XII; 10)', which translated into English reads: 'The righteous care for the life of their animals'.

The fountain remained on that particular site for many years as a focal point but, due to the road improvement scheme to give better access to Clydach Vale via Court Street, it was removed together with the Hairdressing and General Stores of I.G. Locke & Co. Provincial Merchants.

The fountain was relocated on Tonypandy Square to form an island around which the traffic flowed, and it became a well-known landmark in the valley, commonly known as 'The Eros of the Rhondda'. Unfortunately, in September 1958 a car collided with it, knocking it over, and the decision was made to remove it and transport it to the Council Yard at Trealaw for storage until it was decided what could be done with it.

It was found upon examination that many parts of the base fountain section were damaged beyond repair, while parts of 'Our Lady', although damaged, could be repaired.

The statue remained in the Council Depot for many years until it was 'rescued' by the firm of W. Ribbons, Tonypandy. After limited repairs were carried out on 'Our Lady' she was set up on a dressed stone plinth outside the main entrance to their factory where she remained for several years until the closure of the factory.

She was then removed and, in March 1987, placed behind the War Memorial on Dunraven Street, Tonypandy.

It would appear that the statue was removed from its plinth in 1993 for further repair work with the possibility of it being re-sited when the pedestrian area and the traffic bypass for Tonypandy was completed. However, this was not to be, and I believe that the statue is still in storage at the Council Yard in Trealaw.

The main guests and local dignitaries at the unveiling ceremony for the 'Lady with the Lamp' fountain were Dr Gabe Jones, Mr Leonard Llewellyn, both seated, and William Abraham MP. (Mabon) who performed the unveiling.

Tonypandy Square, *c.* 1905. Note the horse-drawn 'taxis' known as brakes which were used to transport people around the area. These were the only vehicles which could travel to Clydach Vale due to the steepness of the surrounding roads

Above: Locals examining the water fountain after its official opening, in October 1909, by Mr W. Abraham (Mabon) MP

Opposite above: Tonypandy Square in 1910. The statue of the 'Lady with the Lamp' is in its original position, and the road at that time is called Llwynypia Road.

Opposite below: View of Tonypandy Square, *c.* 1948. The 'Lady with the Lamp' has been moved to its new position on the Square and acts as an island for the traffic.

The Square Tonypandy   101.

PANDY SQUARE, TONYPANDY

A view of the style leading to Lover's Walk, 1909. The walk was obviously very popular with courting couples at that time!

Demonstration at Tonypandy protesting at the hardship experienced by the public during the 1921 strike.

Tonypandy Square in 1918, dominated by the Pandy Inn (opened in 1861). The inn is still a favourite watering hole with the people of the locality.

St Andrew's Church, Dewinton Fields, 1918.

The interior of St Andrew's Church, c. 1930. In 1988 a restoration fund was set up to carry out repairs to the church. Interior repairs cost £16,000. A total of approximately £50,000 was raised to modernise the exterior of the building and the surrounding walls and grounds.

Theatre Royal, 1910. Note the goods on display outside the various shops. They are now demolished and the land has been converted into a car park. Legend has it that Charlie Chaplin performed here on one of his tours. Local operatic and drama societies also performed on stage, it served as a cinema and boxing matches also took place.

A quiet Dunraven Street in 1906. Note the absence of tram lines.

Dunraven Street, Tonypandy, in 1910, with the locals going about their everyday shopping.

Dunraven Street, Tonypandy, in 1910. Note the gas lanterns above the shop to the left.

A tram proceeding along Dunraven Street towards the Cross Keys and the Empire Theatre in 1912. Note the penny bazaar shop on the left. All goods sold in this shop were priced at one penny, similar to our pound shops of today. Now there's inflation for you!

Another view of a somewhat quiet Dunraven Street, Tonypandy, in 1917.

Above: A quiet Dunraven Street in 1918. The chapel, centre, is now the public library for the area.

Left: Striking miners awaiting the verdict on their comrades on trial at Pontypridd Magistrates' Court in 1911.

A view of Dunraven Street leading to the Empire Theatre, 1918.

A view of Tonypandy from Trealaw in 1909. Note the Pwllyrhebog incline railway (on the left), which transported coal from the Clydach Vale Collieries (top left) down the incline to the main line (bottom left). The open field (bottom right) is now the site of the Tonypandy Medical Centre.

Dunraven Street, Tonypandy, 1923. This was the time when the horses and carts and the trams competed against each other for custom.

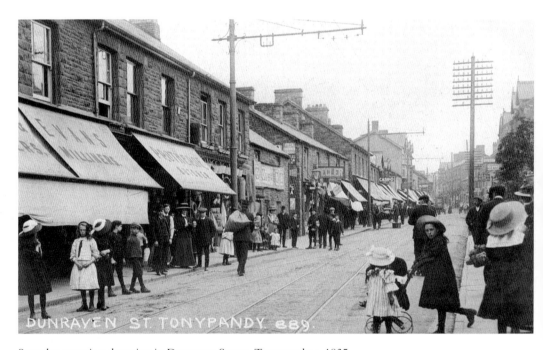

Saturday morning shopping in Dunraven Street, Tonypandy *c.* 1935.

A typical busy scene in Dunraven Street, Tonypandy, in 1935. The car parked away from the tram lines was owned by William Evans of Thomas and Evans, Porth. He was always chauffeured by Mr Tom Griffiths. William Evans' headquarters were at Porth. He was the only large-scale entrepreneur outside of the coal industry, with his Pop factory and his chain of Terry Stores.

A protest march in Tonypandy making its way to Pontypridd during the trial of striking miners in February 1911.

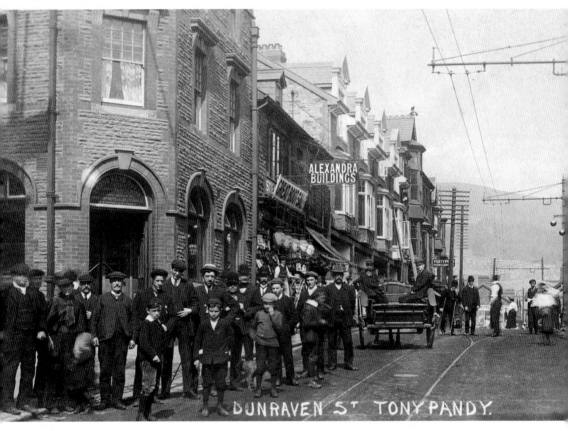

Locals taking it easy outside the Cross Keys Hotel in 1911. The landlord at that time was Mr John Metford.

A typical wet and windy day in Tonypandy, 1918.

Dunraven Street, Tonypandy, in around 1935, with the White Hart Hotel in the foreground (left) and one of the town's trams plying its trade in the distance.

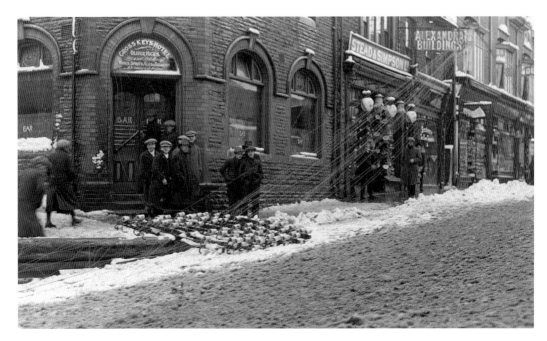

A view showing damage to power lines near the Cross Keys Hotel due to the severe snow storms in March 1916.

Damage to buildings at lower Tonypandy, with power lines and supporting poles collapsing due to the storms at that time.

The New Empire Theatre of Varieties

In the early 1900s, it was realised that the Theatre Royal was very limited in its seating capacity to meet the needs of the expanding population of the time. A consortium from London, together with local businessmen, realised there was a need for a larger and more elegant theatre, with a seating capacity of around 2,000 people. Working in conjunction with local architects and building contractors, they obtained a twenty-five-year lease on a plot of land containing three derelict cottages which were considered an eyesore to an area which, at that time, was undergoing extensive development.

The Empire Theatre of Varieties was built and completed in 1909, and the formal opening of this magnificent building took place on Friday 12 November 1909. Over 100 guests attended a luncheon buffet to celebrate the opening. Mr L.W. Llewellyn ME presided, supported by many local dignitaries, including the main architects of the building, Mr G.F. Ford of Birmingham and Mr J.T. Jenkins of Porth, and the contractors Messrs E.R. Evans & Bros of Cardiff.

At 2.00 p.m. the theatre was formally opened by Miss Annie Morgan, (daughter of the Chairman/Secretary of the Empire Syndicate, Mr William Morgan) by means of a golden key, which had been supplied by the Mirror of Gems, Tonypandy. A programme of musical entertainment then took place, contributed by the mid-Rhondda Orpheus Glee Society, Miss Phyllis Novinsky, the child violinist, and Ap. Tydfil, violinist. A series of living pictures were also shown on the Empireoscope.

The official public opening ceremony took place on Monday 15 November 1909, to a packed audience of approximately 2,000 people. To mark this special occasion, a programme souvenir, printed on silk, was distributed to the audience. The manager of this new theatre (mentioned on the programme) was Mr S.M.B. Hoole. During its heyday, many of the artists who performed at the theatre were either famous or went on to become famous, for example Charlie Chaplin, Jessie Mathews, Tommy Hanley and Arthur English, to name a few.

In the 1940s, films were introduced to supplement the live shows, and this arrangement continued for many years. In the 1960s, Bingo was introduced, but due to the popularity of television at that time and the falling off of attendances, the theatre closed in September 1963 and a new building was erected for F.W. Woolworth, whose shop was officially opened in March 1966. The manager appointed at that time was a Mr Arthur Rees. He presented the first customer of the new store, a Miss M. Jones of Tonypandy, with a tea set with the compliments of the management.

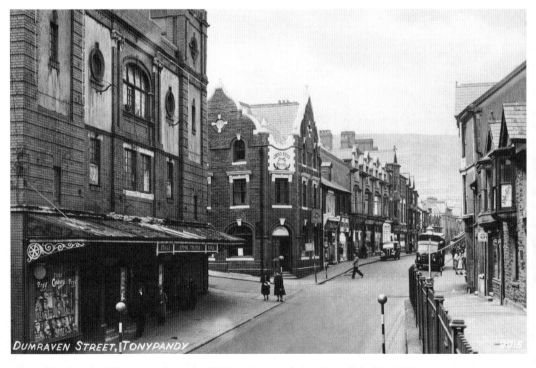

Above: The Empire Theatre in the early 1960s, prior to it being demolished in 1964.

Opposite: The Empire Theatre, Tonypandy, 1910.

STALLS   EMPIRE THEATRE   CIRCLE

HELEN CHARLES

TONYPANDY
EMPIRE

HELEN CHARLES
LAUGHTER & GOLD
RANGERS
& PHYLLIS

BOX OFFICE
SEATS MAY BE
BOOKED HERE

TONYPANDY
EMPIRE

HELEN CHARLES
LAUGHTER & GOLD

The stage and interior of the Empire Theatre, opened in 1909.

Dunraven Street, Tonypandy, 1909. Note the boardings (upper left) on the near completion of the new Empire Theatre.

Dunraven Street, Tonypandy, 1931. The Direct Trading shop was demolished to make way for the new Tonypandy bypass complex, opened in 1987. The Empire Theatre is now the site of Woolworth Stores, which opened in 1966.

A view of Ebenezer Chapel, Tonypandy, in 1910. In its heyday, large congregations were in attendance together with the Cymanfa Ganu, who performed at this chapel.

The ceremony of the opening of the mid-Rhondda Fire Brigade new station at Lower Dunraven Street, Tonypandy, on Thursday 9 April 1908. The ceremony was performed by Mr Kinstley, assisted by Captain F.B. Thomas.

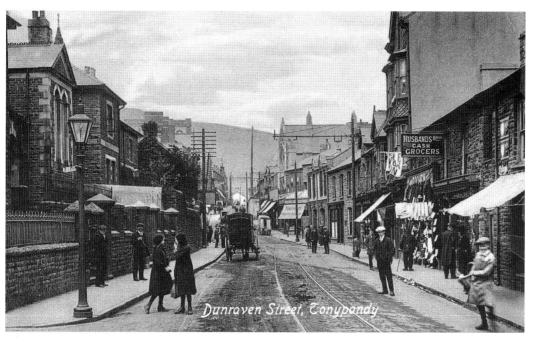

Lower Dunraven Street, Tonypandy, 1914. Note the newly opened fire brigade station on the right, and the horses and carts making their deliveries.

Interior of Ebenezer Chapel, 1911.

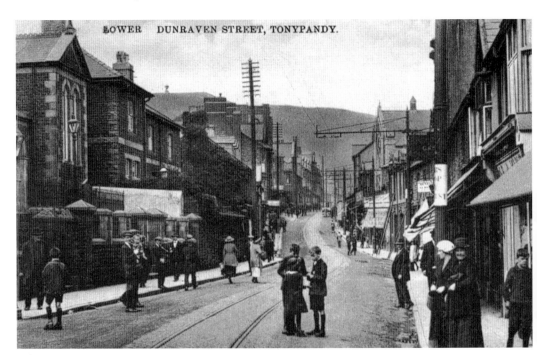

Lower Dunraven Street, Tonypandy, 1913. Note the new Empire Theatre, top left.

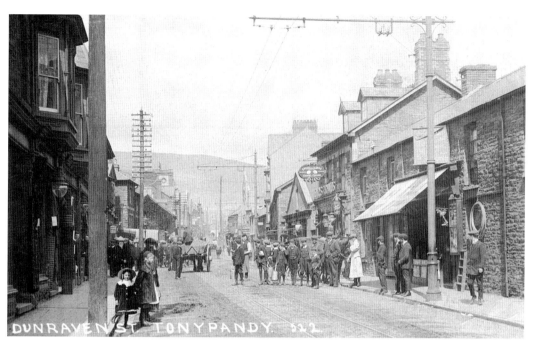

Saturday morning shopping at Lower Dunraven Street in 1910.

A quiet Sunday morning at Lower Dunraven Street, Tonypandy, 1911. The buildings on the right were demolished in 1985 as part of the regeneration scheme for Tonypandy.

Left: A view of the Central Hall in 1931. Demolished in 1985, the site is now being used as a car park for the newly built supermarket in 1995.

Below: Lower Dunraven Street, Tonypandy, 1910. The chapel to the right was demolished and the magnificent building of the Central Hall was built in 1923.

Opposite: A view of Central Hall, 1945, showing the old bridge to Trealaw in the distance. This bridge was demolished to make way for the Tonypandy bypass in 1988.

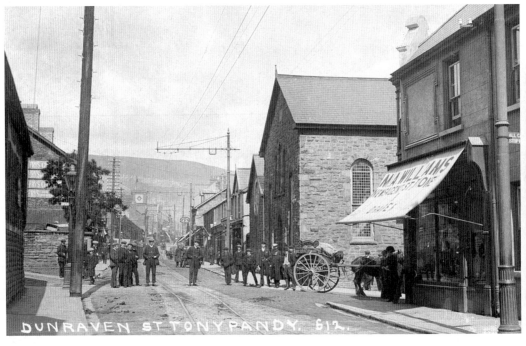

An interior view of Trinity Chapel, built in 1904.

A view of the New Hippodrome in 1915. This was later renamed 'The Plaza' in the heyday of films and was very popular with the local community. However, due to television, attendances declined, it closed and was demolished in the latter part of the 1980s.

The annual chapel outing to the seaside from Tonypandy Station in 1913.

A view of lower Trealaw, with the 'Scotch' Colliery in the distance, c. 1920. The railway bridge to the right (now demolished) was used to transport coal from Clydach Vale via the Pwllyrhebog incline to Cardiff Docks.

A general view of Tonypandy from Amos Hill in 1913. Note the Adare Inn (middle left), now called the Welcome Inn, and the Judge's Hall (middle right).

Naval Colliery, Penygraig, (known locally as 'Pandy Pit'). It was opened in 1875 and closed in 1958, with the power house and stack being demolished in 1962.

four

Clydach Vale

A view of Llwynypia from Clydach Vale in 1906. In the foreground (upper middle) can be seen St Andrew's Church and the stacks of the Glamorgan Collieries.

Thomas Street, Tonypandy, leading to Clydach Vale. Terry Stores, a corner shop, was very popular with the local inhabitants due to the variety of food sold.

Upper Court Street, Tonypandy, 1920. To the left is the Royal Hotel, opened in 1895, and to the right is the road to Thomas Street. Although Court Street was the main road to Clydach Vale, due to its steep incline it was not suitable for the traffic of that time, which used the less arduous route from Tonypandy via Thomas Street, to Clydach Vale.

BLAENCLYDACH · 65144

A view of Blaenclydach showing the 'Monkey Bridge' (now demolished) in the foreground, c. 1956.

Above: In 1863, the Pwllyrhebog incline railway line was built to transport coal from the Blaenclydach Collieries, and later from the Cambrian Collieries to the main line at Trealaw. The gradient of this incline was 1:13, and in 1884 a company called Kitson were commissioned to build the three inclined locomotives Type T.V. Class H, which were numbered 141 to 143. The engines were constructed with their boilers sloping towards the firebox, which ensured that the water in the boiler was always level when travelling on the incline. The wheels were also of a larger diameter than normal to allow clearance over the driving sheaves and ropes. When the railways were amalgamated in 1922, the engines were renumbered 792 and 794.

Opposite above: A view of the bowling green at King George's Park in 1956. The green is still very popular with the locals today.

Opposite below: Peace and tranquillity at King George's Park in the 1980s.

King George's Park and Clydach Vale.

Members of Clydach Vale Bowling Club enjoying a game on a fine summer's evening in 1937. This recreational area, situated high on the side of the mountain, was commonly called 'The Welfare'.

Clydach Road, Blaenclydach, 1956. The large building on the right is the Bush Hotel, a popular watering hole for the local population even today.

A view of Clydach Road, Blaenclydach, in 1906. Transport was provided by horse-drawn passenger brakes due to the steep hills.

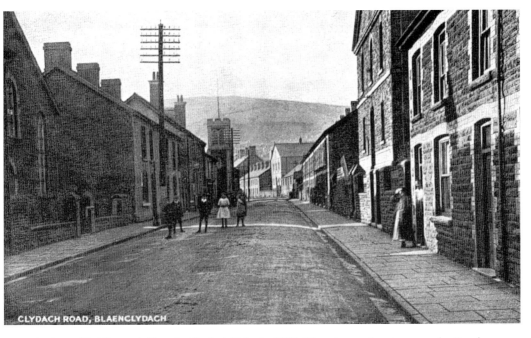

A view of St Thomas' Church, Clydach Vale, in 1908. The vicar at that time was the Revd Williams Meredith Morris. The church celebrated its centenary in 1996.

Riots at Clydach Vale, 1910. In the grocer's shop to the left lived the famous author, Rhys Davies. He described the confrontation between miners and police during this period in his autobiography.

Cambrian Colliery, Clydach Vale, 1905. This photograph was taken after the explosion in which thirty-three miners died.

A view of Cambrian Colliery, *c.* 1910.

Cambrian Colliery in 1919.

St Albans Church situated near to Bush Houses, Clydach Vale, *c.* 1920. Needless to say, the main members of the congregation were from these houses.

A view of Bush Houses in 1964. They were demolished in 1970 as part of the regeneration scheme for the area.

Staff at Cwm Clydach School in around 1933.

Pupils of Cwm Clydach Primary School, *c.* 1933.

A view of the Assembly Rooms (now demolished) and the New Inn Hotel (now a Working Men's Club) in around 1948.

The Square, Clydach Vale, 1907. This was a popular place for the male population to meet at that time.

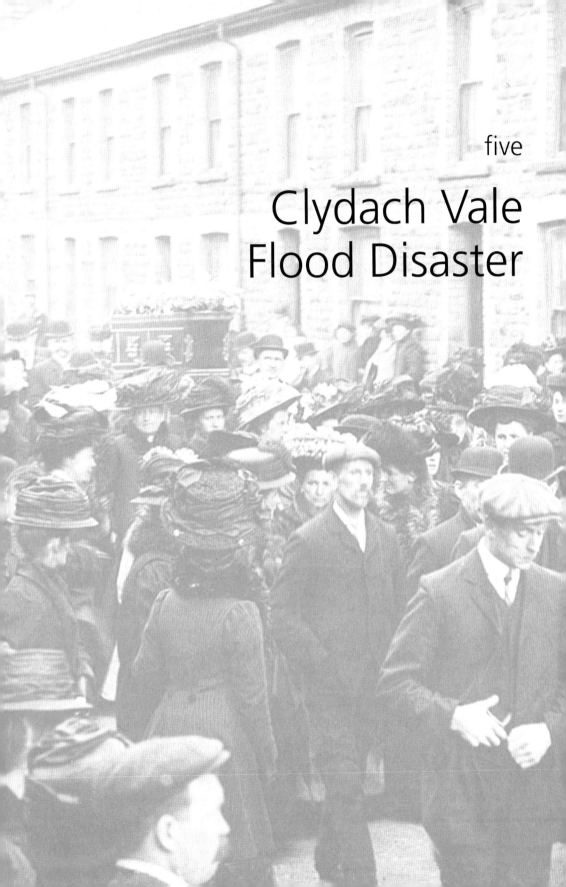

five

Clydach Vale
Flood Disaster

Damage caused by the flood water at Adams Street, Clydach Vale, 1910.

Clydach Vale Flood Disaster

In October 1909, concern had been shown by the residents of Clydach Vale about rumours circulating regarding a large accumulation of water in the old Ffynondwym Level, named after the farm on whose land it lay. This level was also known as Perch Level (William Perch of Cardiff had sunk the level in 1847). The level had been abandoned about five years previously, the No.2 Rhondda seam having been worked. Due to this local concern regarding the water build-up, workmen employed by Messrs Pugh and Thomas, building contractors, Tonypandy, were, at approximately 4.00 p.m. on that fateful Friday 11 March 1910, engaged in 'tapping' the ground around and in the level to relieve the accumulation of water through various outlets. Simultaneously other building operations, including the digging out of channels, were being carried out near to the entrance of the level to control the movement of the discharging water. The residents of houses in the immediate vicinity had been warned of a possible rush of water from the level which would result from the 'tapping' operations. No one involved in this work fully appreciated the mass of water that was being held by the barrier, or the resulting tragedy and the loss of life that would occur later that day. The people of Clydach Vale, on that cold and damp day typical for that time of year, were going about their normal daily tasks, and were totally oblivious to the terrible tragedy about to befall them.

Without any warning, the mountainside seemed to suddenly give way as though from an eruption, and a torrent of water together with masses of earth, mud, and boulders of various sizes swept down the hillside with such terrific force that it carried the contractors' equipment before it, and caused the workmen at the level to run for their lives.

The released water, later estimated to be no less than 800,000 gallons, together with the accumulation of earth, mud and boulders, surged forward, demolishing everything in its path. In Adams Street, which was situated near the level, six houses were completely wrecked, and the entire street numbering about fourteen houses was flooded to a depth of up to 5ft of water.

The gutted house in Adams Street caused by the flood water.

In the heart of the village, directly in the path of the torrent, stood the local school. The headmaster, Mr R.R. Williams, was present in No.1 classroom when he saw the rushing flood of water coming down between Saron Chapel and Dr. R. Gabe Jones' house.

Immediately, he realised that the old level had burst. Within what appeared to be only seconds, the wall dividing the school from the roadway was breached and the flood water came rushing into the school yard and the classrooms. Mr Williams's first thought was to secure the safety of over 900 children who were in the school at that time.

The boys, due to the position of their classrooms, were able to be taken out in an orderly manner by Mr D.R. Rees, an assistant teacher. It was impossible to get them out of the building by the main entrance as this led to the flooded playgrounds, so a large number were passed over the playground wall into the nearby lane which led away from the flood waters to relative safety.

The girls' school, however, was invaded by the raging flood water, which had demolished the front door of the school and destroyed the lower parts of the windows. The water was rushing in with terrific force, carrying with it huge blocks of timber, wreckage from the houses which had been destroyed and also from the level itself.

The interior of the school was devastated inasmuch as the furniture of the school, that is the cupboards and even the school piano, were floating in the flood water, and the desks were all smashed by the force of the water and carried away by the raging current.

The lives of many of the children were seriously threatened by these events. Fortunately, the tragedy was avoided by the heroic efforts and selflessness of a large number of colliers who were walking home after finishing their shift at the local colliery. They immediately responded by wading up to their waists and even up to their armpits in the mud and flood water to enter the Girls' School. They secured planks, ladders and other makeshift materials through the damaged school windows and, with the help of the teachers who were in the building and other passers-by, succeeded in rescuing the children by assisting them along the makeshift gangways into the boys' playground which then led to safety.

Due to the immense pressure caused by the large mass of water present in the yard, the wall at the bottom of the playground finally gave way, and with this barrier removed, the flood water quickly dispersed down the railway incline and into the river, and undoubtedly saved many young lives.

Mr David Rees, the assistant teacher, commented later that, as far as the school was concerned, it was fortunate that the disaster occurred at that particular time when the colliers were passing near the school on their way home from work. It if had occurred at any other time it would be too dreadful to contemplate what might have happened.

Unfortunately, despite the gallant efforts of all concerned, three of the schoolchildren were drowned. They were Blodwen Davies, Enid Howells and Gertrude Rees. The other unfortunate victims of the disaster were Mrs Elizabeth Ann Williams and her infant daughter Francis, and the infant boy Haydn Brimble, all from Adams Street. In all, the flood claimed six victims, details of which are as follows:

Mrs Elizabeth Ann Williams, aged thirty-four years, and her infant daughter Francis (Fanny) Williams aged ten weeks, of 9 Adams Street, Blaenclydach.
Haydn Brimble, aged three weeks, of 10 Adams Street, Blaenclydach.
Blodwen Davies, aged nine years, of 4 Howard Terrace, Blaenclydach.
Enid Howells, aged six years, of 64 Wern Street, Blaenclydach.
Gertrude May Rees, aged five years, of 39 Marion Street, Blaenclydach.

For further information on this disaster, refer to the publication *Clydach Vale Flood Disaster, 1910*, by David J. Carpenter.

Victims of the flood disaster of March 1910 being taken to the Llethr-Ddu Cemetery at Trealaw on Wednesday 16 March 1910.

Procession of mourners making their way to the cemetery at Trealaw. Notice the coffin of one of the child victims being carried shoulder high.

The interior of the classroom badly damaged by the flood waters.

The school walls collapsed through the sheer force of the flood waters.

The entrance of the level after the flood waters had receded.

A view of the level area, together with the sheds of the mining engineers who were investigating the cause of the disaster.

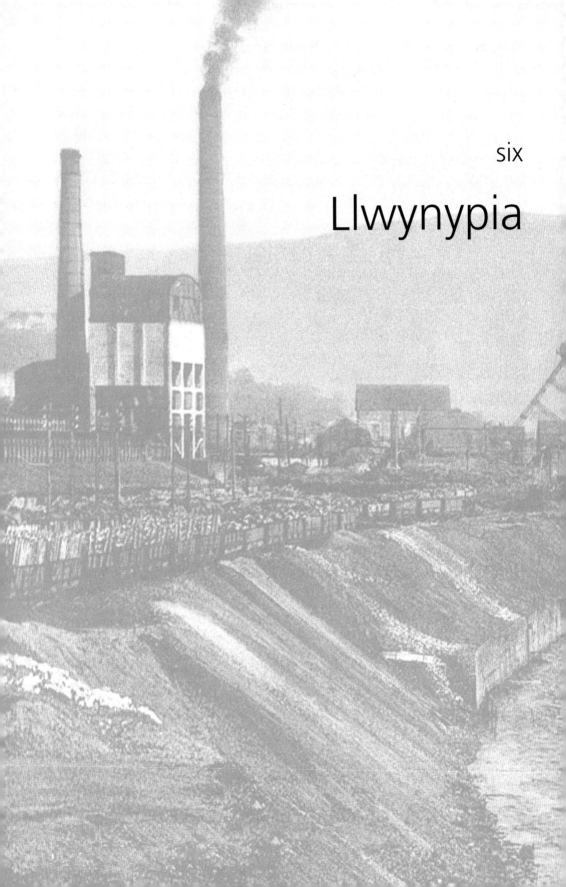

six

Llwynypia

Pupils of Llwynypia Infants' School in 1927. Their teacher was Miss Williams.

Above: Pupils of Llwynypia School who had sat their exams for the Rhondda Higher Education Scholarship in 1932.

Opposite: Members of the Tonypandy and Llwynypia Unemployment Club at 26 Berw Road, in 1937. Among them are: Sid Moore, David 'Dai' Carpenter, and Gwilym 'Gyw' Williams. The club was known locally as the 'Sprig and Hammer', due to the amount of carpentry that was produced there.

Archibald Hood

After the death of Archibald Hood in October 1902, it was decided that a fitting memorial to his life be erected. The high esteem in which he had been held by his employees was evident, in that it was they who suggested that such a memorial be erected, and in effect contributed £600 towards it. It was therefore only fitting that the first statue in the Rhondda should be erected to the memory of Mr Archibald Hood in the grounds of the Llwynypia Library and Institution. The statue would be life-and-a-half size, 7ft 6ins in height, and cast in bronze, the sculptor of the statue being Major Walter Merrett of London. The statue depicts Mr Hood with outstretched arm pointing towards the Glamorgan Collieries. The pedestal, which is in Aberdeen and Cornish granite, was executed by Mr R.S. Griffiths of Tonypandy, and bore the following inscription on the front: 'This statue is erected by his workmen and friends as a token of respect to his memory'. This inscription is also inscribed on the rear in Welsh.

The day of the unveiling was fine and sunny and, with it also being Federation Day, resulted in large crowds assembling for the unveiling ceremony. Many distinguished guests were present for the unveiling, some of the more distinguished being Messrs W.W. Hood and Thomas A. Hood (Mr Hood's sons), Leonard W. Llewellyn (agent of the Cambrian Colliery, Clydach Vale), Doctors David and Llewellyn, W.P. Nicholas (Clerk of the Council), Alderman Richard Lewis JP and Councillors R.S. Griffiths, D.C. Evans and L.P. Griffiths, to name a few. The principal guest speaker was Mr W. Abraham (Mabon) MP. In unveiling the statue, Mr Abraham said that they were gathered together for rather a unique event in the history of the Rhondda. This was the first statue erected to any man outside of those in the local cemeteries, and it afforded him the greatest pleasure in being asked to come there as their representative to unveil the statue on their behalf. To those gathered, Mr Hood was known not as an employer of labour alone, but as a friend of the working man, and predominantly as a man of peace. He then led the vast crowd in the singing of O fryniau Caersalam ceir gweled to the famous hymn-tune Crugybar.

STATUE OF THE LATE ARCHIBALD HOOD ESQ

The statue of Archibald Hood, erected in front of the Llwynypia Miners' Library and Institute in 1906 (now demolished). It was unveiled by William Abraham (Mabon) MP.

Mr W.W. Hood then spoke with considerable emotion. It was extremely difficult, he said, for him to express what he felt on his own behalf and on behalf of his brother and sister. Words failed him, and he could only thank them for perpetuating the memory of a good father and a good employer. To this there was loud applause.

Mr Thomas A. Hood also expressed under considerable emotion his sincere gratitude for the kindness shown to the memory of his father, and the proceedings concluded with the singing of the Doxology.

Llwynypia House in 1904. It was converted into the Cambrian Lodge NUM Social Club in August 1964 and is still popular with the locals today.

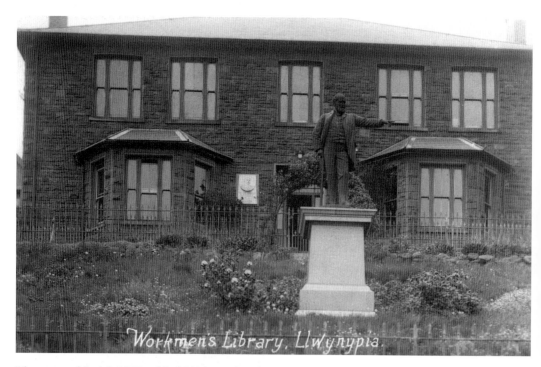

The statue of Archibald Hood in 1910 located in the grounds of the Miners' Library and Institute. It was built in 1878 and demolished in 1994.

Headstone of the tomb of Archibald Hood at Cathays Cemetery, Cardiff. (ref. M559/M536).

A close-up view of the inscription on Archibald Hood's headstone.

Glamorgan 'Scotch' Colliery, 1914. Note the 'Mansion' at top left, home of Leonard Llewellyn, manager of the Cambrian Collieries.

The colliery in its heyday in 1904.

Glamorgan 'Scotch' Collieries, 1930. Note the miners' cottages (called the terraces) situated around the colliery workings, and the incline (middle right) used to transport the waste to the tip situated on the mountain.

GLAMORGAN COLLIERY,
LLWYNYPIA

Glamorgan 'Scotch' Collieries, *c.* 1933. Note the No.6 shaft to the right.

A view showing the new factories built on the reclaimed site of the Glamorgan 'Scotch' Collieries, *c.* 1952. Note the shaft of the demolished No.6 Colliery in the foreground.

A view showing the cluster of miners' cottages situated around the Llwynypia 'Scotch' Collieries in 1927.

GENERAL VIEW, MIDRHONDDA.

Sold by G. Jones, Newsagent.

A view showing the 'Scotch' Terraces built by Archibald Hood to house the miners who worked at the Llwynypia 'Scotch' Collieries in 1960.

A view of Llwynypia in 1935, showing the Glamorgan 'Scotch' Colliery in the distance.

Left: Pontrhondda Farm, *c.* 1906. The tenants at that time were Mr and Mrs John. The farm was demolished in 1907 due to the roof being blown off during a storm.

Below: Rhondda College of Further Education in 1960.

Above: The 'Homes', 1921. Originally built as a Union Workhouse in 1903, it became the 'Homes' in 1911, and became a hospital in 1927. This was the first general hospital in the Rhondda.

Below: The bowling green at Llwynypia, *c.* 1960. This green was very popular with the people of the area, and was situated near to the Llwynypia Railway Station.

Llwynypia Hospital, 1936. In the 1970s the hospital added 195 beds for the treatment of patients, together with a modern outpatients and casualty department, which is still serving the community today.

A general view of Sherwood, Llwynypia, 1922. Note the 'mansion' on the left and the open field on the right. This was later developed as a small factory site, creating employment for the local community. It is soon to be developed as the site of the new Rhondda Hospital.

seven

Glyncornel
House

Glyncornel House

Archibald Hood, the founder of the Glamorgan which opened in 1861, resided for a short period at Gilfach Coch (known locally as Hood's House) and then later the Sherwood House, Newport Road, Cardiff. However, his son William Walker Hood, who became the General Manager of the Glamorgan Collieries, resided at Hen Glyncornel (Old Glyncornel) which is situated at the right of the estate as you enter the main gates.

However, further up the mountain, a larger residence to be known as Glyncornel House (the mansion) was to be built on a much grander scale. This was to be the residence of Mr Leonard W. Llewellyn, the General Manager of the Cambrian Collieries, who in later life received a knighthood for services to the community. The house was built with bricks from the Glamorgan brickworks; the date of its construction is not known, but from information received of that time it appeared to be in the very early 1900s.

The area surrounding the house at that time was approximately seventy-five acres. The drive leading up to the house curved around it, and a bridle path leading to the stables was located through the grounds. A cobbled courtyard was situated at the imposing front entrance to the house. The area surrounding the house was made up of croquet and tennis lawns, together with a large orchard and vegetable garden, while the remainder was laid out as lawns and pathways. A large lake stocked with a variety of fish together with breeding ponds is situated at the lower part of the estate. Once past the imposing entrance, the main feature within the house was the impressive main staircase, which enhanced the character of the interior of the house.

In 1939, the Rhondda Borough Council took over the grounds and the house. During the war years of 1939–1945, the main building housed evacuees who had social and behavioural problems and could not be billeted with local families. The house narrowly escaped damage by German bombs which fell in the Rhondda in April 1941.

After the war years, with the departure of the evacuees, the house was used as a maternity hospital. However, in 1959 it was converted to a geriatric hospital, and remained as such until 1979.

L.W. Llewelyn, esq, 1874–1924.

From 1981, the Borough Council transformed the house in order to accommodate a variety of organisations who were coordinating as a Tourist and Educational Establishment. An Environmental Study Centre has been established, and local schools and various adult groups have worked on a number of interesting projects as the house and grounds lend themselves to opportunities for historical, geographical and ecological studies to be carried out.

Through a joint scheme, the Rhondda Borough Council has been able to negotiate with the Youth Hostel Association (YHA) to establish a sixty-bed hostel at Glyncornel. The YHA is now totally established at this centre, and many young people from many countries have enjoyed their stay at the centre and have not only taken advantage of the facilities at the centre, but have got to know the people of the Rhondda.

Fifty-five acres of the grounds have been leased to the Pentref Bowmen, who have hosted British and European Archery competitions over the last few years. The large lake, which is regularly stocked by the Authority, is leased by the Glyncornel Angling Association.

In all, the Glyncornel Complex has a large range of activities to suit all groups and interests, something we should be proud of and not take for granted. It is still used for a great variety of projects today.

Hen Glyncornel, 1909, the home of William Walker Hood, general manager of the Glamorgan Collieries. He was the elder son of Archibald Hood, owner of these collieries.

The grounds of Hen Glyncornel in 1904. In later years, a substantial part of the grounds was sold off and a private housing estate built.

Glyn-Cornel, Lake Llwynypia.

A view of Llwynypia, *c.* 1960. Note Glyncornel Lake in the foreground.

Glyncornel Lake, Llwynypia.

A view of Glyncornel Lake in 1912. Situated on the estate of Mr Leonard W. Llewellyn, general manager of the Cambrian Collieries, it was a popular choice for members of the gentry at that time to enjoy weekends of hospitality and entertainment with such activities as fishing, shooting, etc.

Above: The Prince of Wales at Glyncornel House, home of Sir Leonard Llewellyn, in 1919, meeting with local dignitaries.

Opposite: Extract from *Who was Who* Vol. 2 1916–1928.

LLEWELYN, Sir Leonard (Wilkinson), K.B.E., cr. 1917; late Controller of Non - Ferrous Metals, Ministry of Munitions; b. 11 June 1874; s. of late Llewelyn Llewelyn, J.P., High Sheriff, Monmouthshire, 1918, and d. of Geo. Wilkinson; m. 1st, 1899, Edith (d. 1913), d. of late Edward Jones, J.P., D.L., of Snatchwood Park, Pontypool, Monmouthshire; one s. three d.; 2nd, 1922, Mrs Elsie Louise Jones, Glen Usk, Caerleon, Newport, Mon. *Educ.*: Monmouth Grammar School; Cheltenham; Heidelberg; Officer of the Legion d'Honneur; Officer of the Order of Leopold; Officer of the Order St. Stanislav; Silver Medal of the Royal Humane Society; High Sheriff Monmouthshire, 1920; J.P. Cos. Glamorgan and Monmouth; Director of Duffryn Aberdare Colliery Co. Ltd., Cambrian Collieries, Glamorgan Collieries, Fernhill Collieries, John Lysaght, Ltd., Sankey and Sons, Ltd., Harwood Bros. Ltd., Phœnix Patent Fuel, Ltd., Arrow Fuel, Ltd., Consolidated Cambrian Collieries, D. Davis and Sons, Welsh Navigation Colliery Co., Managing Director of North's Navigation Collieries (1889) Ltd., Celtic Collieries Ltd., Crown Preserved Coal Co. Ltd., Frenchwood Mill Co. Ltd., and other large steel and colliery undertakings; contested North Monmouthshire General Election, 1918. *Recreations*: polo, horse-breeding, golf. *Address*: Malpas Court, Newport, Mon.; Glen Usk; Caerleon, Mon. *T.*: Newport 2887. *Clubs*: Junior Carlton, Bath, Sports. *(Died 13 June 1924.)*

Ffynon Fair. (Mary's Well). Penrhys.

Gelligaled Swimming Pool, Ystrad-Rhondda.

Above: Further up the valley from Glyncornel House is St Mary's Well, Penrhys, seen here in around 1902. Its waters were reputed to have healing powers. It has been the scene of many pilgrimages by religious bodies over the years.

Left: Bathing 'belles' at the outdoor swimming baths at Gelligaled Park in 1954. The baths closed in 1975 when the new sports centre opened.

Tyntyle Hospital, 1977. It was originally built for the treatment of infectious diseases.

The Isolation Hospital was built in 1887, consisted of a four-bed ward, and was known as the Ystradfodwg Cottage Hospital. It continued to treat infectious diseases until 1972, and closed in 1991. It reopened in 1994, and was renamed the Rhondda Nursing Home.

Other local titles published by Tempus

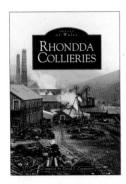

Rhondda Collieries
DAVID J. CARPENTER

When King Coal came to Rhondda he changed the face of the valley forever. Where sheep and small farming communities had dotted the hills, a multitude of collieries and industrial working towns sprang up. By 1911, 42,000 men and boys were employed in Rhondda's fifty-three collieries. This compilation is a vivid record of the valley's mining heritage, from the daily working of the mines to the sudden tragedy of pit disasters.
0 7524 1730 4

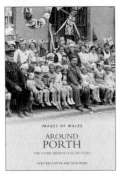

Around Porth Stories behind Porth
ALDO BACHETTA AND GLYN RUDD

This book captures the essence of community life in Porth during the last century, with images of farmers ploughing fields, soot-covered miners and local shops and businesses. We recall the local people who have lived and worked in Porth, adding to its vibrancy and bustle. Memories of royal visits, street parties, clubs and societies are relived through striking images and memories of Porth's rural character.
0 7524 2496 3

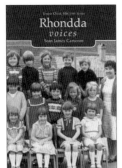

Rhondda Voices
SEAN JAMES CAMERON

'We all rushed to the church hall and waited with baited breath to see exactly what "evacuees" were...' This collection of memories records life in the Rhondda valleys from the late nineteenth century onwards. Drawn from a wide variety of sources, it includes often humorous anecdotes of everyday life from local people, notes from the diary of a surveyor prospecting for coal and extracts from the log book of the National School.
0 7524 2625 7

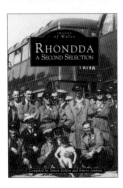

Rhondda A Second Selection
SIMON ECKLEY AND EMRYS JENKINS

Both the Rhondda Fach and Fawr have fallen on hard times through the closure of their mines. Through illustrations of the miners' strikes, this book explores the economic difficulties faced by many. In times of trouble, however, a strong community spirit remained, and people are also shown at leisure, in sporting clubs, in choirs and in bands. This book depicts the many aspects of life in the Rhondda Valley.
0 7524 0308 7

If you are interested in purchasing other books published by Tempus, or in case you have difficulty finding any Tempus books in your local bookshop, you can also place orders directly through our website

www.tempus-publishing.com

or from   **BOOKPOST**, Freepost, PO Box 29, Douglas, Isle of Man, IM99 1BQ
tel 01624 836000   email bookshop@enterprise.net